LASTING FREEDOM

BOOK ONE

HEART HEALING SERIES

Growing in Grace Publishing
Chattanooga, Tennessee

In association with Torn Curtain Publishing
Wellington, New Zealand
www.torncurtainpublishing.com

© Copyright 2023 Vikki Waters. All rights reserved.
ISBN Softcover 978-0-6453977-9-6
ISBN EPub 978-0-6457827-0-7

No portion of this book may be reproduced, stored in a retrieval system or transmitted in any form or by any means—electronic, mechanical, photocopy, recording or otherwise—except for brief quotations in printed reviews or promotion, without prior written permission from the author.

This book is not intended as a substitute for professional counseling or medical advice.

Unless otherwise noted, all scripture is taken from the New International Version®, NIV®. Copyright © 1973, 1978, 1984, 2011 by Biblica, Inc.™ Used by permission of Zondervan. All rights reserved worldwide.

Scripture quotations marked NASB are taken from the New American Standard Bible®, Copyright © 1960, 1971, 1977, 1995, 2020 by The Lockman Foundation. Used by permission. All rights reserved. lockman.org

Scripture quotations marked TPT are from The Passion Translation®. Copyright © 2017, 2018 by Passion & Fire Ministries, Inc. Used by permission. All rights reserved. ThePassionTranslation.com.

Scripture quotations marked MSG are taken from THE MESSAGE, copyright © 1993, 2002, 2018 by Eugene H. Peterson. Used by permission of NavPress. All rights reserved. Represented by Tyndale House Publishers, a Division of Tyndale House Ministries.

Scripture quotations marked TLB are taken from The Living Bible, copyright © 1971 by Tyndale House Foundation. Used by permission of Tyndale House Publishers, Carol Stream, Illinois 60188. All rights reserved.

Typeset in Baskerville Display PT and Palatino

Cataloging in Publishing Data
    Title: Lasting Freedom
    Author: Vikki Waters
    Subjects: Christian Living, Spiritual Life, Personal Growth, Spiritual Growth, Christian Ministry, Discipleship, Inner Healing, Counseling, Prayer, Spiritual Warfare

LASTING FREEDOM

TAKING BACK YOUR AUTHORITY IN CHRIST
IN EVERY AREA OF YOUR LIFE

DR. VIKKI WATERS

DEDICATION

I dedicate this *Heart Healing Series* to my Growing in Grace tribe who have pressed in to partner with Father, Jesus, and Holy Spirit to experience deep and lasting freedom. Our journeys together have ignited a passion for helping others experience the same. We are raising an army of trained and equipped Heart Healers with proven and effective tools to bring sustainable transformation to the Body of Christ. God desires His much-loved sons and daughters to walk in more excellent emotional health, free of negative mindsets, and confident in knowing who they are, whose they are, and what they carry.

Special thanks to the various streams of inner healing I have gleaned from over the years. I have gained much from your examples and ministries and made it my own as I have walked it out personally and given it to others. We are building on the foundation you have laid.

I also dedicate this series to my children and grandchildren; your Honey and Papa have plowed the hard ground and become the first in our family lines to declare no more generational bondage, cycles of lack, poverty mindsets, and destructive patterns – it is over – it will not continue. Instead, we embrace the truth and reality of the abundant life and live powerfully because of what King Jesus has done for us, in us, and through us, through His death and resurrection to life. We pass this torch to you – our ceiling is your floor for generations to come!

CONTENTS

Introduction		1
PART 1: UNDERSTANDING YOUR FREEDOM		3
Chapter 1	The Doorway of Decision	5
Chapter 2	How We Give Our Power Away	13
Chapter 3	Knowing Your New Identity	19
Chapter 4	Jesus Has Made You Powerful	27
PART 2: CLOSING THE DOORS TO THE ENEMY		31
Chapter 5	The Door of Sexual Sin	35
Chapter 6	The Door of False Religion and Idolatry	43
Chapter 7	The Door of Hatred and Anger	51
Chapter 8	The Door of Fear and Control	59
A Letter from Vikki		69

INTRODUCTION

Have you ever felt dissatisfied? Unable to shake the sense that this isn't all God intended for you? Deep within most of us is a desire for the abundant life Jesus spoke of in John 10 but there's a gap between our experience and what He promised that we aren't quite sure what to do with. We long for a greater connection with the Father, with Jesus, and with the Holy Spirit, but instead find ourselves in a secret struggle with destructive sin patterns that we can't figure out how to fully break free from. And so, we create distance between ourselves and God because we wrongly believe that He is displeased with us because of this bondage.

I want you to know from the outset that you are not alone in these struggles. I also want you to know that the 'more' you have been longing for *is* possible. In each of the six books in this *Heart Healing Series* you will discover the heavenly realities you *already* have access to as a lavishly loved child of God. These realities will enable you to stop looking for love and significance in all the wrong places and empower you to make good choices.

This is the issue: we *believe* in freedom, but generally speaking, we don't know how to steward it well; we don't know how to *choose* it. But the death and resurrection of Jesus position us and empower us to discern what is best *and* to choose it. When we truly recognize who we are, *whose we are*, and how Jesus has equipped us for the abundant life, we can't help but pursue that kind of joy and lasting freedom in every area of our lives.

One of the things that will help us in this pursuit is understanding the two types of doors that exist in our lives: the destructive doors of the enemy, and the door of the Father's love. In this book, we will explore these, learning to make good choices at each 'doorway of decision' so that we can close doors that rob us of the abundant life and step into the door of the Father's love where we can discover the 'more' He intended for us all along.

PART ONE

UNDERSTANDING YOUR FREEDOM

1

THE DOORWAY OF DECISION

Have you ever felt like a fraud? I know I have. Even years after becoming a Christian and a full-time minister I continued to struggle with destructive patterns, so much so that at one point I told my husband I needed to leave full-time ministry because I felt like such a hypocrite. Here I was, teaching the Bible and coming alongside other people to help them find healing, while still so broken and in deep pain myself. I felt stuck. I didn't know my true identity as a child of God, and so, despite my vocation, I was operating with an 'orphan' mindset.

I remember the angst that arose in me one day towards two of my Christian colleagues. I felt offended, rejected by them. In reality, they weren't rejecting me, but because I filtered the situation through a lens of pain, that was how I interpreted their actions. The results were disastrous. My 'stinking thinking' caused me to behave in ways that were hurtful to both myself and others, and I fell headlong into an emotional ditch of my own making. Instead of owning my responsibility to take my thoughts captive, I chose to self-medicate and isolate myself for protection. Little did I know that, in doing so, I opened doors to the enemy that allowed him to wreak even more havoc in my life.

The prodigal son we read of in Luke 15 was very familiar with this way of operating. Not content with what was available to him in his father's house, he cashed in his inheritance early and indulged in some rather 'wild living' in his search for greener pastures (v. 13). We could also think of it as 'addictive living'—like when people self-medicate through escapism or excess, only to end up bound by the very thing that was meant to bring relief. When we think of addiction, our minds usually go to substances such as alcohol and drugs, or illicit activities like pornography and gambling. But addiction can take many forms. Anything from food, to sleep, to work, to television or social media or video games . . . even exercise or relationships can become a source of addiction when they occupy the wrong place in our lives.

To the prodigal son, the wild, addictive life seemed greener. It seemed somehow better and more exciting, to the point where he was willing to leave the safety and security of his father's house to pursue it. Unfortunately, we can be prone to do the same. We too find ourselves attracted to, and quickly falling into, self-destructive behaviors—despite our past experiences of God's love. More often than not, the reason the illusion of greener pastures fools us is rooted in one of two heart problems: unhealed pain in our hearts, or an unmet core need for love. Left unaddressed, these heart issues create an opening for the enemy that he takes full advantage of.

DOORS FOR ENEMY ACCESS

When we are wounded, it's as if a little place in our souls becomes broken or crushed. The more pain we experience, the more broken our hearts become. The accumulation of pain begins in our very early years. The wounds we are inflicted with may come at the hands of others, or they may be the result of our environment or circumstances. Sometimes, in attempting to make the pain stop, we even hurt ourselves further. We self-medicate in one way or another, then wind up in terrible bondage, wondering how to end the constant turmoil in our hearts.

Thankfully, Jesus can heal our hearts—it's His specialty! He is the One who came to bind up the brokenhearted (Isaiah 61:1). But so often we try everything *except* turning to Jesus for healing! I personally wasted years of my life self-medicating for a variety of reasons. The first was that I was afraid of being vulnerable. Past experience made me wary of opening my heart up to others and trusting them with it. My filter of unhealed pain told me that it was too risky, that to trust could only lead to judgment, betrayal, and further wounding.

Connected to this was my fear of rejection. I thought that if people knew the real me—if they knew about both my past and my present struggles—they would not like me. So, I rejected people before they had a chance to reject me. And, as funny as it may sound, I just couldn't imagine my life without pain. It was so familiar to me that even though it wasn't helping or working for me, there was a degree of comfort in staying stuck in it; it was what I knew.

Albert Einstein brilliantly defined insanity as doing the same thing over and over, expecting different results. There came a point where I had to make a choice as to whether I would continue to leave the door open to the enemy or partner with Jesus to bind up my wounds and allow the Father to minister love into my very core, thereby casting out fear once and for all.

It may seem like a contradiction to say that a believer can have an unmet core need for love. *How can we experience the gift of salvation, yet still need something more?* The answer is simple: If we struggle to *believe* God loves us personally and unconditionally, we will struggle to *feel* the love He has towards us. We are all designed to receive and be filled to overflowing with the love of God. But until we learn how to have a genuine relationship with Him, our longings will go unsatisfied, leaving us trying desperately to fill the void on our own.

This is particularly true when we have had legitimate needs go unmet at some point in our lives. For instance, as children, we expect our parents to provide for us and keep us safe, guiding and instructing us as we grow. We expect that home will be a place of nurture where we can experience companionship and find comfort. If this is not the case, we may develop a belief that we need to assume responsibility and take charge of meeting our own needs in those areas. This often results in a desire for control which causes fractures in our relationship with Father God, Jesus and the Holy Spirit, as well as in our relationships with others. When this is perpetuated, we become stuck in a cycle of lack. This is where we get to make a pivotal decision: *Will we open a door to the enemy, or choose to walk through the door of the Father's love?*

THE DOORWAY OF DECISION

When we receive Christ, we are supernaturally transferred from the kingdom of darkness into the Kingdom and family of God. Satan no longer controls us (Colossians 1:9–14). We have become citizens and inheritors of a heavenly Kingdom, with access to *all the blessings and security that brings. However,* many Christians allow the pain of their past to not only limit their relationship with God but also to prevent them from living out this new reality. Because of this, they are susceptible to the enemy's lies.

The truth is, the enemy cannot snatch us away from our Father (John 10:27–30), but he can lie to us about who we are and what will satisfy our hearts. He tries to persuade us to wander from our Father and live as though we are still citizens of darkness, promising that the excesses and addictions of a 'wild life' will meet our heart's cry. We need to understand that *when we listen to his voice, we give our authority away.* In other words, our agreement with the enemy empowers his lies and leaves us vulnerable to his attack.

This is what happened with Cain in Genesis 4. When God accepted his brother Abel's offering but not his own, Cain fostered a heart of anger and jealousy towards Abel—to the point of scheming his murder. God spoke to Cain and pointed out that he had a choice to make, saying:

> *"If you do what is right, will you not be accepted? But if you do not do what is right,* **sin is crouching at your door***; it desires to have you, but you must rule over it."*
> Genesis 4:7

Cain was at the doorway of decision. Two choices lay before him: one good, and one destructive. He could either believe God and do the right thing, or he could lean on his own understanding and act on his anger and, in doing so, come into agreement with the enemy's lies. Unfortunately, he chose the latter, and sin was all too eager to spring into action the moment Cain gave away his power.

The prodigal son also faced a doorway of decision. When he left his father's house to pursue his own desires, he became vulnerable. He gave his power away to the enemy through his agreement that the grass was greener away from home. Through that open spiritual door, the enemy brought famine and poverty into his life. The enemy didn't break down the door; the son's choices permitted him to walk through it.

Here's what we need to learn from the lives of Cain and the prodigal son: *Believe in your freedom and learn how to make right and better choices through the power of Jesus living within you!*

The enemy cannot force us to believe his lies. The son did not need to go to a far country, and neither do we. When we are tempted to sin and pursue satisfaction outside of God's will, God has already provided, at the doorway of decision, the ability to say no. The apostle Paul made this clear when he wrote:

> *No temptation has overtaken you except what is common to mankind. And God is faithful; he will not let you be tempted beyond what you can bear. But when you are tempted, he will also provide a way out so that you can endure it.*
> 1 Corinthians 10:13

We can always choose to stay close to the Father's heart, allowing Him to wrap us in His protective embrace as we trust His healing work in our lives. All we have to do is turn to Him, and He will help us recognize the truth about our situation and empower us to make good choices. When instead we choose to wander from God's heart, it becomes harder and harder for us to acknowledge the truth about God and ourselves. Our minds are flooded with lies, our emotions become a mess, and we begin to hate ourselves, imagining that our Father also hates us. Yet the Father always holds open His door of love. No matter what we may do, that door remains open to us. He is a good Father!

For us, the doorway of decision, as with Cain and the prodigal son, is simply an invitation to return to the lavish love of our Father. When we choose to receive that love and step into deeper relationship with Him, we begin the journey to true freedom.

Let me tell you my testimony: *The day I finally said no to sin and yes to God, was when I really started growing.* As I came to understand the truth of my identity in Christ and all that He has given me access to as His child, my choices and behavior began to change. At this powerful door of decision I chose, and continue to choose, to believe that what God says about me is true. It takes intentional practice. We must STOP, EVALUATE, and CHOOSE. In doing so, we are making new habits that will lead to lasting freedom. Not just a temporary freedom or a quick fix, but a reality as you become a powerful overcomer in that area.

THE VOICE OF LOVE AND LIFE

Since hearing the voice of God is so essential to our healing, it's important that we know how to discern His voice from that of the accuser. This is especially important as we come to the door of decision. *How can we tell them apart?* James, the half-brother of Jesus, tells us that God's wisdom is always, "pure; then peace-loving, considerate, submissive, full of mercy and good fruit, impartial and sincere," bringing a beautiful harvest of righteousness and spiritual maturity in our lives (James 3:17-18). And because God is love (1 John 4:16), His words are also filled with love. In His love, He has given us the Holy Spirit to be our friend, counselor, and tutor. Even when He is correcting us and disciplining us, His voice will always sound like love and bring life.

The accuser's voice is the exact opposite and will always be one of condemnation. His words have a mission to kill, steal, and bring destruction into your life. The enemy wants to get your focus off Jesus and onto your problems. He desires to bait you with hopelessness and confusion about your identity so that, even as a believer, you remain living out of an orphan mindset. Thanks be to God, you, my friend, are no longer an orphan under the control of this voice of accusation. You are a child of the King, and you know what His voice of love and life sounds like. Keep your ears tuned to Him!

THE DOOR OF INTIMACY WITH GOD

In Revelation 3:20, Jesus extends an invitation to us saying, "Here I am! I stand at the door and knock. If anyone hears my voice and opens the door, I will come in and eat with that person, and they with me." Many have interpreted this verse to be an invitation for salvation, however, if you look closer at the context, you will see that Jesus is speaking to the *believers* in Laodicea. They had become distracted by their wealth, and as a result, their love and passion for Jesus had become lukewarm. Jesus is inviting them to pursue true riches, to listen to His voice and open the door of their hearts to enjoy fellowship with Him.

Jesus tells the believers in Laodicea that if they decide to accept His invitation, His love will cover their shame, their passion will be reignited, and their spiritual blindness removed. Not only that, He promises to empower them to be overcomers, reminding them of where they are spiritually seated: on the throne with Him at the right hand of the Father (Revelation 3:8-21). This invitation—this door to His presence and all that accompanies it—is always wide open for the believer to walk through.

One image which always helps me say yes to Jesus' offer of intimacy and fellowship is found in Revelation 4:3. There we read that God's throne is surrounded by green light—a rainbow that shines like an emerald encircles it! Anytime I want to enjoy a deeper connection with Him, I envision myself seated next to Him in this life-giving light. This rainbow also reminds me of God's grace and mercy to Noah after the flood. It is the same grace and mercy that enables us today to close the doors to the enemy and instead open our hearts to receive Christ's love.

If you find yourself standing at the doorway of decision, it's time to choose which way you will go. I urge you to say yes to God and step into the fullness of what He offers you.

2

HOW WE GIVE OUR POWER AWAY

Imagine your life is one big room filled with doorways. Some doorways will lead you into the abundance God has for you, while others, if opened, will leave you vulnerable to the enemy's attack.

What can we do when we look around and realize the wrong doors have been opened? We must close these destructive doors and reclaim our authority. When we listen to the accuser's voice at the doorway of decision and come into agreement with his lies, we give away authority—we actually *give him permission* to bring misery into our lives. He is not forcing these doors open; we have opened them for him, giving him the legal right to wreak havoc in our lives.

Thankfully, there is good news: Jesus has defeated him—not in part, but in full. And as we learn to walk in the victory and freedom Jesus has gloriously given us access to, we are able to take back our authority, boot the enemy to the curb, and deny him access to our life.

In order to effectively do this, however, God's voice must become the one we listen and respond to. We must stand firm in the truth of all that He says and determine to stay in agreement with Him. In so doing, we can not only close these destructive doors, but ensure they *stay* shut.

DOORS OF DESTRUCTION

In order to close the doors that give the enemy access to our lives, we must first understand what these devastating doors are. The apostle Paul gives us a clear picture of them in Galatians 5:

> *Now the deeds of the flesh are evident, which are: sexual immorality, impurity, indecent behavior, idolatry, witchcraft, hostilities, strife, jealousy, outbursts of anger, selfish ambition, dissensions, factions, envy, drunkenness, carousing, and things like these.*
> Galatians 5:19-21a (NASB)

Within these verses, we see four different categories of sin:

- *Sexual sin and soul ties*: sexual immorality, impurity, and indecent behavior.

- *False religion and idolatry*: idolatry and witchcraft.

- *Hatred and anger*: hostilities, strife, jealousy, outbursts of anger, selfish ambition, dissensions, factions, and envy.

- *Fear and control*: drunkenness, carousing, and things like these.

When we engage in any of these behaviors, we open the door to the kingdom of darkness. In order to close them, we must identify not only who we have come into agreement with, but also the specific lies we have believed.

Repeated patterns of sin become strongholds in our life. But sometimes, because of the protection we believe that habit or person offers us, we don't always recognize them as a stronghold. For example: pornography can pose as a form of comfort; drugs and alcohol can pose as a means of escape; and eating disorders and lying can pose as a form of control. But make no mistake, these only offer counterfeit protection.

In order to find freedom from destructive patterns, we need to be willing to ask ourselves some hard questions. Questions like: *How is this working out for me? What is this sin doing for me? Am I miserable enough yet? How desperate am I for a better life? Is this where I want to be in twelve months, three years, or ten years from now—stuck in the same struggles?*

I don't believe anyone truly wants to stay stuck in patterns and behaviors that don't serve them well. It certainly isn't God's heart for you—that's why Jesus went to such lengths to secure a better life for you. If you will allow Him to, He will help you take back your authority and power, tear down these strongholds, and close these doors for good!

BEHAVIOR MODIFICATION IS NOT FREEDOM

It's likely if you're reading this book that you have already attempted to find freedom. Perhaps you've worked with accountability partners, read self-help books, attended twelve-step groups, received professional counseling or therapy, installed online filtering software, or even resorted to snapping rubber bands on your wrist! Throughout the centuries, Christians have tried many methods to stop destructive behaviors, only to find limited or temporary freedom. When they find themselves reverting back to their old ways, discouragement inevitably sets in.

The emphasis on behavior modification is that you *do* something to *get* something, which leads to *forming your identity around your actions and behaviors*. While some of these tools are helpful, they are not enough in and of themselves. This is because your identity is not meant to be based on what you can do, but on what has already been done for you. Jesus is the author and perfecter of your faith (Hebrews 12:2), He is one hundred percent committed to your wholeness, and the truth is, He has already done *everything* needed to set you free.

The only effective path to lasting freedom is found in having the correct perspective of your new identity. How you view yourself must be centered on the New Covenant and grounded in the finished work of Christ. While the Old Covenant emphasized adherence to the law, focusing on works and behavior, that is not the covenant you and I live under this side of the cross. The cross does not represent behavior modification but rather a brand-new identification! The New Covenant Jesus forged in His blood makes us a new creation. We do not need to try and earn His love or approval, or add to what He has done; His sacrifice was once for all (Hebrews 10:14), and when He declared, "It is finished" (John 19:30), the war against sin was won. And because He has triumphed over sin and death, you can too.

YOU ARE POWERFUL TO MAKE RIGHT CHOICES

All believers will experience temptation. That is a given. But it is not a given that you need to be overcome by those temptations. Over the years, I've come to understand that our ability to resist the enticement to sin is rooted in how we perceive our identity. We either believe that we are powerful in Christ and that the finished work of Jesus has made it possible for us to say no to sin, or we believe that we are powerless victims fighting the devil around every bush and corner. Sadly, too many Christians believe the latter, and the result is misery, exhaustion, and hopelessness; they understand freedom as a concept, but live not knowing how to choose freedom as a reality.

Until we learn how to be transformed through the renewal of our minds, standing firm in the truth of how God now sees us, we will continue to wrestle with sin. If we think we are a wretch, a worm, and a sinner, then we will sin by faith!

Jesus did not set you free from the bondage of sin so you could continue to struggle. That is the work of the enemy. He is set on stealing from you and destroying Christ's work in you, but Jesus came to give you "everything in abundance, more than you expect—life in its fullness until you overflow!" (John 10:10 TPT). He came so that you might experience the reality of abundance and lasting freedom in *every* area of your life. Any area that is marked by the enemy's destructive work needs an immediate upgrade in your thinking. The way that you perceive who you are and respond to temptation needs to change.

It is time to learn the value of your freedom and to take responsibility for it. At the doorway of decision, God's grace has made you powerful to say no to sin (Titus 2:11-12). If you are struggling to do this, Peter writes that if we lack godly qualities in our behavior, it is because we have forgotten that we have been "cleansed from our past sins" (2 Peter 1:9). Apparently, the solution for believers who sin is to remember who we are and more fully celebrate that we are forgiven.

It's important to understand that if Jesus had *just* died, we would still be forgiven. Under the Old Covenant sacrificial system, once a year the High

Priest would enter the Most Holy Place to offer an unblemished lamb as an atonement sacrifice for Israel's sins, *yet not one of those sacrificial animals rose back to life. Not one!* This means that the resurrection of Christ accomplished something more than just the forgiveness of our sins—not only were we washed clean, but our identity and position in life was fundamentally changed.

When you became a Christian, you received this costly freedom, a new identity with right standing with God, and forgiveness of every sin. Not only that, Jesus seated you with Him in the heavenly realm at the right hand of the Father (Ephesians 2). That is your permanent position. That means you are already as close to Jesus as you will ever be this side of heaven!

Let that truth sink in for a moment. As humans we tend to think we have to do things to get closer to God. *Have a consistent quiet time. Keep short accounts of forgiveness towards others. Tithe ten or more percent. Read your Bible every day.* This is a performance-based mindset to get something we already have. But as believers, we cannot do anything to get any closer to God than we already are. Our position in Christ is secure, and now our task is to make life-filled decisions that reflect the truth of our new identity. To do that, you must be convinced that *what is true of Jesus is true of you*. You no longer have to fight *for* victory. Instead, you can stand firm and respond to life *from* His victory over sin, death, and the enemy.

As we stand firm in the completeness of the Father's forgiveness and love for us, see ourselves as a new creation empowered by the Holy Spirit to make right choices, and live from heavenly realities, we begin to value our freedom and take responsibility for it.

The message of resurrection life through Jesus is the best message on the planet. *Will you choose to align yourself with everything God says about you? Will you choose to believe that what is true of Jesus is true of you, my friend?* I pray that you will experience rest, freedom and victory on a daily basis as you embrace this identity shift.

3

KNOWING YOUR NEW IDENTITY

Have you ever watched old cartoons where a character has a demon and an angel perched on either shoulder, offering them counsel? They find themselves torn between two worlds, wrestling with whether to choose good or evil. Sadly, this is how many believers feel. They see themselves as being caught in a lifelong battle between two natures resident in them, and as a result, they spend their whole lives trying to do what Jesus has already done.

Romans chapter six makes it very clear, however: Your old self has been crucified with Christ (v. 6). It died and cannot be resurrected. It is gone, which means you are no longer a slave to sin, "because anyone who has died has been set free from sin" (v. 7). But not only are you to "count yourself dead to sin" (v. 11), you are also to recognize that you have been raised with Christ to live a new life (vv. 4&12). While Jesus' death dealt with who you once were, His resurrection made you into something new! Your old, deceitful heart is gone, and you have been given a new heart. But to effectively live out this new identity in your Christian life, it is essential that you understand that *your death was an event, and is not a process.* This means you do not need to take up your cross and die daily.

Unfortunately, most believers have been taught to fight with the flesh, take up their cross, and die daily. Let me say it again: they see themselves as being caught in a lifelong battle between two natures resident in them, and as a result, they spend their whole lives trying to do what Jesus has already done.

This teaching that we must take up our cross comes out of Luke 14:25-33 where Jesus, speaking to His *potential* followers, tells them, "Whoever does not carry their cross and follow me cannot be my disciple" (Luke 14:27). He was cautioning *unbelievers* to count the cost of becoming His disciples. But to rightly interpret His words, we need to understand what they meant in the first century. To 'take up your cross' was to be willing to lay down one's reputation and be branded by society as a criminal. Jesus Himself would later die a criminal's death on the cross, something that was considered cursed by the Jewish people, and He was making it clear that those who chose to become affiliated with Him must also be willing to lay down their reputation and become rejects of society.

Jesus was *not* talking here about how to win the battle against the flesh by applying His cross to your life. This teaching has often been taken out of context. At your salvation, you identified with the cross of Jesus, burying your old self with Christ so that He could resurrect you as a brand new person. You took up the cross once, and it is a *past tense event, not an ongoing process.* Praise God!

Similarly, Paul's words in 1 Corinthians 15:30-32, where he wrote that he faced death daily, have often been misconstrued. Paul was *not* talking about crucifying the flesh every day to be more like Jesus; he was describing the horrible persecution he faced for following Jesus—the beatings, stonings, incarcerations, and possible executions. Jesus was crucified *once*. You were crucified with Him, *once*. It is a done deal.

Too many believers spend their lives trying to *do* what Jesus has already *done*, believing that they are supposed to defeat what He has already defeated for them, instead of simply receiving and dwelling in Christ's victory. I lived many years from this place, and it was exhausting. When I finally decided to believe the truth about my new identity and what Jesus has accomplished for me, I stopped fighting with myself and began a beautiful journey to healing and wholeness.

We must be willing to let go of misconceptions no matter how long they have been taught, and allow the Spirit of God to renew our minds regarding these essential truths so that we can enter into the fullness of what God has prepared for us.

THE NORMAL CHRISTIAN LIFE

The truth that the death of your old identity as a sinner is a past event and *not* a present process, means sin is no longer a part of your struggle. In fact, the New Testament writers didn't even expect Christians to sin! In 1 John 2:1-2 (TPT) we read:

> *You are my dear children, and I write these things to you so that you won't sin. But if anyone does sin, we continually have a forgiving Redeemer who is face-to-face with the Father, Jesus Christ, the Righteous One. He is the atoning sacrifice for our sins, and not only for our sins but also for the sins of the whole world!*

John expected believers to walk a sinless life; the "but if" of this passage was merely a backup plan. Yet this is not the expectation that many of us carry. We feel like Paul, when he wrote, "I have the desire to do what is good, but I cannot carry it out. For I do not do the good I want to do, but the evil I do not want to do—this I keep on doing" (Romans 7:18-19). *But is Paul really suggesting here that a constant struggle with sin is the normal Christian life?*

Many have inaccurately taught from Romans 7 that Paul experienced an ongoing fight on the inside between his old identity and his new spirit. This has led people to erroneously believe that Paul was unable to do the good he wanted because he was a slave to the power of sin living in him—and if the apostle Paul couldn't do good, then who are we to think that we can do better?!

However, when we look at the surrounding chapters, we see that Paul was not writing of a present struggle. He was contrasting his old life subject to the law with his new life subject to the Spirit. Paul clearly teaches about the victory of grace over sin, rejoicing that sin's reign is finally over and we are no longer slaves to sin, but to righteousness (Romans 6:6, 17-18). Right in the middle of Paul's explanation of the new life in Christ, he hits the pause button with chapter seven, to insert a testimony of what his life *used to be like* as a slave to the law and to the power of sin. Before Jesus rescued him from the kingdom of darkness, he was completely enslaved to the power of sin, wanting to do good but unable to do so on his own. Having set up this contrast of what life looked like prior to being raised with Christ, he then picks back up in chapter eight to elaborate on the joy and freedom of this new life led by the Holy Spirit.

Remember that, while many Christians have found comfort in relating to Romans 7, even going so far as to excuse living in sin, this was no longer Paul's reality. Paul was using contrast to make a point: *Being enslaved to the power of sin is not the normal Christian life. Being in step with the Spirit is.*

YOUR KINGDOM BENEFITS PACKAGE

The truth is, as a believer, you are no longer at war with yourself. You are a new creation with everything you need to live out the new life God has opened to you. You have a "Kingdom Benefits Package"!

Firstly, as we have already seen, God performed a *radical heart surgery* on you at the moment you received Christ, ripping out your wicked, deceitful heart of stone and replacing it with a *new heart* which has a constant, undying, eternal love for Him (Ezekiel 36:26; Ephesians 6:24). This new heart is wired and fueled by the Holy Spirit to walk with Him in obedience and dependence on His truth (Romans 6:17).

But a new heart is not the only thing that God has given you. He has also supplied you with a *new mind*, the mind of Christ (1 Corinthians 2:16). This means you never again have to say, "but what if my thoughts are not His thoughts?" Your thoughts now discern God's thoughts, and you are able to hear His voice clearly.

He also gave you a *new nature*, one that is fully alive with the character and nature of God. You now have His DNA—everything you will ever need for a life of godliness has been deposited deep inside you. He calls you intimately by name to partner with His goodness and His promises as lavishly loved sons and daughters (2 Peter 1:1-4).

In addition to your new nature, you have a *new spirit* that aligns with Him (1 Corinthians 6:17); you were taken out of Adam and birthed into Christ (Romans 5:12-21, 2 Corinthians 5:17). This was essential to make you compatible with Jesus. Jesus is not the new creation—you are! You were born a sinner, but your re-birth now defines you as a child of God. You are Christlike in this world (1 John 4:17). *Certainly, you are a saint who sometimes sins*, but rest assured His Spirit is training your new spirit to live like Jesus.

As you go on this journey of learning to live out of your new identity, the Holy Spirit is your counselor and guide, the One who leads you into all truth (John 16:13). He is your source and your strength. And as you lean into Him, He will renew your mind, empowering you to walk brilliantly and confidently. The Holy Spirit is committed to your wholeness, healing and maturity, and it is His delight to live on the inside of you.

My friend, I strongly encourage you to embrace these truths of how incredibly blessed, valued, and significant God has made you. All three members of the Godhead were involved in making your resurrection life possible—that's how much they love you. It's time to see yourself how you're seen in heaven, to live like you are bonded to Christ. He is a person, and in relationship with Him you can confidently be yourself! You get to express Jesus and the 'real you' at the same time, with no conflict.

DO THE MATH AND BE EMPOWERED

Many verses in the New Testament talk about putting off the old and putting on the new. This progressive process of becoming more like Jesus is often referred to as 'sanctification'. It's where we learn, grow, and mature in Christ.

In Romans 6:11, Paul tells us to, "count yourselves dead to sin but alive to God in Christ Jesus." To 'count' comes from a bookkeeping term that means 'to acknowledge, reckon, or rely on a fact'. We must acknowledge and rely on the fact that we are dead to sin. The old person we once were, is dead and gone. Count that truth as a fact! Then *count* yourself alive to God! Practically speaking, through your new identity, you can now choose to say no to the old behaviors, cravings, attitudes, and ways you used to live and think.

As God's masterpiece, His work of art (Ephesians 2:10), our regenerated lives are not the problem. Sin is the problem. You are dead to sin. Sin is not in you—sin comes from outside of you. Our calling is to say no to sin and say yes to who we truly are (Romans 6:12-14). We cannot be in sin and express Jesus at the same time. So, quench sin, walk in the power of the Spirit and express Jesus.

We are all practicing something. Doctors practice, lawyers practice, and believers practice too! It is in our 'practice' that as growth and transformation take place, we begin to experience ever-increasing glory (2 Corinthians 3:18). When you say *no* to temptation, you can say *yes* to God with bold confidence, *yes* to your new life, *yes* to making good choices. It will take time and practice for you to make this your new norm, but soon you will begin to do it more effectively. And the more often you successfully say yes to the new you, the more these strongholds will lose their power in your life.

Practice is what enables us to learn and grow into mature sons and daughters. As you practice living out of your new identity, the internal conflict and confusion will give way to peace, joy, and fruitfulness.

SPIRITUAL WARFARE IS ALWAYS ABOUT YOUR IDENTITY

It's true, and the Bible makes it very clear: Spiritual warfare will always be about who you believe you are. Let me give you two striking examples.

In Genesis 3, Eve was tempted by the serpent in the garden of Eden to eat from the tree of the knowledge of good and evil. He told her that she would be like God when she ate from the tree. Here's what Eve should have said in response to this temptation: "Look here, you revolting deceiving serpent. I'm already like God because I am made in His image. Now, get out of my garden and don't come back!" What a difference that response would have made.

Apparently, Eve got confused during her confrontation with the serpent. At the doorway of decision, she lost sight of her true identity. Eve gave her power away to the enemy with her choice to sin, *when she didn't have to*. The enemy suggested that God was holding out or withholding from her, or that she wasn't enough and she needed to *do* something to be like God. And she fell for the accuser's lies about her identity.

Did you know that before the fall, Eve did not have a nature that was enslaved to sin? She had the power to make good or bad choices based on what she believed about her identity. She is a *perfect example of a believer now*. We don't have a sin-nature either because we are in Christ. We have been given the ability to make good choices and take responsibility for our freedom because that's how much God values us!

In Matthew 4, Jesus was also confronted by the accuser. This event came on the heels of Jesus' baptism. There, His Father clearly affirmed His identity when He said, "This is my Son, whom I love; with Him, I am well pleased" (Matthew 3:17). While Jesus was in the wilderness, Satan challenged Jesus' identity three times saying:

> *If you're the Son of God, then turn these stones into bread . . . (v. 3)*
>
> *If you're the Son of God, then jump from this building so the angels can catch you . . . (v. 6)*
>
> *If you will bow down and worship me, I will give you all the kingdoms of the world . . . (v. 9)*

Each time, he was calling Jesus' identity into doubt.

But Jesus knew who He was, and was assured of His Father's love for Him and approval of Him. At the doorway of decision, Jesus rejected the accuser's lies. Like Eve, He was tempted, but unlike her, He modeled for us how to confidently respond to the accuser's voice and lies. And in doing so, He demonstrated this truth: Spiritual warfare will always be about who you believe you are.

YOU ARE SIGNIFICANT IN THE KINGDOM

It is essential that you are grounded in what God says about you; you must know who you are, whose you are, and what you carry. What you believe about these things will either lead to abundant life or misery. *Are you a sinner? Or are you powerful to choose self-control? Are you enslaved to sin? Or are you seated with Christ as a new creation?*

Next time you are tempted, stand firm and respond from victory. Declare out loud: "No! That is not who I am anymore! Sin is beneath me. I am not under the power of the enemy and I refuse to give my power to him by believing his lies. I choose to say no to temptation and yes to my new creation identity. God has made me powerful! I value my freedom, and the Spirit empowers me to take responsibility for my freedom. Accuser, get out of my garden and don't come back!"

4

JESUS HAS MADE YOU POWERFUL

I've said it before and it's worth repeating: It's time to see yourself how you're seen in heaven, to live like you are bonded to Christ. He is a person, and in relationship with Him you can confidently be yourself! You get to express Jesus and the 'real you' at the same time, with no conflict. When you truly know your significance in the Kingdom you will walk in confidence, keeping the doors to the enemy firmly closed and the door to God wide open.

Paul wrote this to the young believers in Galatia:

> *At last we have freedom, for Christ has set us free! We must always cherish this truth and stubbornly refuse to go back into the bondage of our past . . .*
>
> *Beloved ones, God has called us to live a life of freedom. But don't view this wonderful freedom as an excuse to set up a base of operations in the natural realm. Constantly love each other and be committed to serve one another.*
> *Galatians 5:1, 13, TPT*

You have been set free entirely from the power of sin, and the wages have been paid (Romans 6:23). Past. Present. Future. Jesus died and paid it all. There are no more wages left. So let's do the math and celebrate!

If such great freedom has been purchased for us, why would we ever want to continue to sin? In the words of Titus 2:11- 14 (TPT),

> *God's marvelous grace has manifested in person, bringing salvation for everyone. This same grace teaches us how to live each day as we turn our backs on ungodliness and indulgent lifestyles, and it equips us to live self-controlled, upright, godly lives in this present age . . . Jesus, the Anointed One . . . sacrificed himself for us that he might purchase our freedom from every lawless deed and to purify for himself a people who are his very own, passionate to do what is beautiful in his eyes.*

Here's the bottom line: God has equipped you to take responsibility for your freedom. When we realize that the Spirit of God empowers us to confidently resist every temptation to sin, we will do it more effectively. It takes practice. Practice allows us to learn and grow into mature sons and daughters. Our calling as new creations, tethered to Jesus, is to say no to sin and yes to who we truly are. In doing so, we will take back our authority, keep the doors to the enemy closed, and enjoy lasting freedom in every area of our lives.

SIT DOWN WITH JESUS

Did you know that among the furniture in the Jewish temple there was no chair? A priest in old testament times would never sit down on the job! And yet, in Hebrews 10:11-12 we read:

> *Day after day every priest stands and performs his religious duties; again and again he offers the same sacrifices, which can never take away sins. But when this priest had offered for all time one sacrifice for sins, he sat down at the right hand of God.*

Do you see the contrast? In the Old Testament, the priests had to remain standing because their work was never done. Day after day, they had to offer the same sacrifices which could never take away sins. Jesus, however, did the unthinkable. He offered just one sacrifice, once and for all. Then He sat down, because His work was finished.

Jesus' finished work means we too can stop—there is no need for us to run around trying to get forgiven or stay forgiven. God invites us to sit down with Jesus! He wants us to agree that the once-for-all sacrifice of Christ was enough and nothing else needs to be done. You are forgiven completely, perfectly, and forever. You can relax and enjoy your new creation life because the sin issue between you and God is over!

STAY IN THE CHARIOT WITH JESUS

Colossians 2:13-15 (MSG) says,

> *When you were stuck in your old sin-dead life, you were incapable of responding to God. God brought you alive—right along with Christ! Think of it! All sins forgiven, the slate wiped clean, that old arrest warrant canceled and nailed to Christ's cross. He stripped all the spiritual tyrants in the universe of their sham authority at the Cross and marched them naked through the streets.*

When Paul wrote this to the believers in Colossae, he had a significant picture in mind: If a Roman General had a notable victory, his army would march through the city in celebration. The general would ride in his chariot, followed by a procession of the kings and leaders he had defeated. Stripped naked, chained, and openly branded as spoils, these defeated foes were pulled behind the conquering general in a show of public humiliation.

Jesus did the same exact thing to Satan and the kingdom of darkness after His resurrection! He stripped the enemy of all his power and authority, parading him openly as a defeated foe. Consider that picture for a moment. Today, King Jesus is our conquering hero! He is in the chariot, and Satan is defeated!

Now picture yourself in the scene. *Where are you?* You are in the chariot with Jesus! You are safe and secure. You are seated close beside Jesus—the One who is both righteousness and victorious! You share in His spoils! You have the authority to enforce His triumph in every area of your life (2 Corinthians 2:14)! You never need to stop the chariot so you can talk to or rebuke the enemy. You only need to laugh at him. You are the lavishly-loved child of the conquering King!

~

I pray that you feel greatly encouraged by these truths. They are game changers in our spiritual journey. I wish I had learned them earlier. Whenever my mind and emotions are in a mess, it is because I have lost sight of my identity in Christ. But when I lean back and rest in Jesus, the Holy Spirit reminds me who I am and whose I am. He empowers me to value my freedom, take responsibility for it, make the right choices, and walk in triumph because of His resurrection victory.

It is the same for you, my friend! God knows who you are. Your job is to agree with Him and live from your new creation life! You are powerful to make good choices. Stay in agreement with what God says is true about you and your circumstances. Let's close the destructive doors in our lives and keep them closed. How? By staying in agreement with God at the doorway of decision. By remaining in the chariot with King Jesus. By valuing our freedom and taking responsibility for it. By choosing the abundant life Jesus already has secured for us.

PART TWO

CLOSING THE DOORS TO THE ENEMY

When we come to the doorway of decision and choose to engage in sinful behaviors, we open the door to the kingdom of darkness. We give legal right to the enemy to interfere in our lives. In a sense, we are partnering with the demonic. This hinders our intimacy with God. The good news is that we have the authority and ability to close that door once more and in so doing, restore our intimacy with the Father, Son, and Holy Spirit.

To do this, we must identify the open door, deal with it through the finished work of Jesus, shut the door, and make room for the Holy Spirit to work in our lives. As we explore this process in these next four chapters, you will have an opportunity to close each door and take back your power.

Before you get started, let me say this: When you ask Jesus to reveal where and how the spiritual doors in your life were opened, it is *imperative* that you listen only to Him and keep your focus on what He highlights for you. The aim isn't to go rooting around for every sin and mistake. Remember, all your sins are forgiven. Instead, the goal of this personal ministry time is to gain your breakthrough by closing the doors as Jesus reveals what He wants to deal with. Jesus promises to meet you on any path of pain and lead you back to His glorious, everlasting way—the path that brings you back to Him (Psalm 139:24, TPT). Life more abundant is always His goal for you!

When you reach the end of each chapter and are ready to close that specific door, I encourage you to take your time. Find a comfortable place, get some paper, a pen, and perhaps some Kleenex. As you work through each question, ask yourself what you sense Jesus highlighting to you and note it down. You can be confident that He will help you close every door to the enemy and discover the door of love. It's time to take back your power!

5

The door to
SEXUAL SIN

Inside this door can be found: *perversion, lust, adultery, pornography, masturbation, abortion, fantasy, sex outside marriage, homosexuality, lesbianism, transsexualism, satanic ritual abuse, lewdness, unwholesomeness, molestation, rape, abuse, violence, impurity, sexual immorality, indecent behavior, shame, betrayal, judgment, hopelessness, depression, control, and unforgiveness.*

As humans, we are created for intimacy. We are designed to be nurtured and strengthened in community. God's intention was that we find and experience healthy connections within our marriages, families and friendships. Ultimately, He wired our hearts to find fulfillment in Him. Until we believe and embrace this foundational reality, we will look to other people and things to meet our legitimate needs. And when we try to meet our need for intimacy in unhealthy or ungodly ways, we can find ourselves opening the door to sexual sin and creating unhealthy ties to other people.

OPENING THE DOOR TO SEXUAL SIN

Before we consider how this first door gets opened, let's define what is meant by 'sexual sin'. It is not simply 'sex outside of marriage', as some might say. The Bible takes a much broader view. In Matthew 5:28, Jesus had this to say about immorality:

> *But I tell you that anyone who looks at a woman lustfully has already committed adultery with her in his heart.*

Jesus holds up the measuring line regarding sexual sin in our thought life! Whether we are thinking it or doing it, if it is directed outside the covenant relationship, it is sin. We cannot afford to place the line anywhere else, nor can we pick and choose what is safe to get away with regarding our sexual purity. Denial is a dangerous choice that only leads to misery.

There are many ways that the door to sexual sin can be opened. You may have suffered sexual abuse or trauma, opening a door that was not of your choosing. Or perhaps you have felt like something is wrong with you or that no one could ever truly love you, and this has caused you to compromise and accept less than what God desires for you. Maybe someone showed you pornography when you were a kid, or you felt lonely at some point and clicked on a website, and it led you further and further down a path of darkness and addiction. Or perhaps you had an affair. You may even have swung this door open wider, thinking it was too late to go back. However, the door to the enemy was opened, and you have the power to close it again.

Whether the door to sexual sin opened through our own doing or because of something that happened to us, we are wounded as a result of that opening. The accuser takes advantage of our pain, feeding us lies and temptations to comfort us. But his comfort is always a counterfeit of the true and lasting comfort the Father wants to offer us.

This doorway of decision will either lead to life or to further pain. When we participate with the enemy's schemes in the area of sexual perversion and sin, he gains access to many areas of our lives. One of the ways that he does this is through soul ties.

THE FORMATION OF SOUL TIES

You won't find the phrase 'soul ties' in Scripture; it is a modern term used to describe the connections formed between people and can have both healthy and unhealthy connotations. In healthy relationships, we learn to *bond*. We discover how to be emotionally available, connected, and physically intimate in ways appropriate to the relationship. However, when the relationship is unhealthy and sin is involved, we do not bond. Instead, we become emotionally and physically *bound*, creating an ungodly soul tie.

Healthy connections provide safety for both parties. In godly relationships, there is a commitment to work through difficulties—and to do so without attacking one another or taking offense. Instead, you encourage one another, believing the best without being blind to where growth is needed. Like Jonathan did for David, you promote and spur each other on, each looking out for the interests of the other. Yet you do not suppress yourselves; you are strong *together* rather than at the expense of the other.

In contrast, unhealthy connections tend to rob people of their strength and individuality. When another person is given too much authority over you, or you end up in co-dependency, you are allowing yourself to be manipulated and controlled by another. Sometimes you even begin to mirror that person's mood and health, or are unable to make decisions without them. Fear that someone will be upset or punish you, or even leave you, stops you being yourself. You may also feel that their problems are your fault or responsibility. Even if you have left the relationship, you may find yourself thinking about that person obsessively, having recurring dreams about them, and being unable to commit to another because of the hold they still have on you. You may also find yourself repeatedly returning to them in spite of abuse. This indicates the likelihood of an unhealthy soul tie.

Scripture is clear that one of the ways an unhealthy soul tie is formed is through sexual sin. In 1 Corinthians 6:16 (TLB), Paul tells us:

> *And don't you know that if a man joins himself to a prostitute, she becomes a part of him, and he becomes a part of her? For God tells us in the Scripture that in his sight the two become one person.*

What a confronting picture! We become a part of *every* person that we are sexually intimate with. Within marriage, this is a godly joining—a symbol of the covenant we have entered into with that person. Outside of that context, unhealthy soul ties are formed, and until those ties are severed, we remain connected to that person or persons. Their open doors become our open doors, and ours, theirs. This is a sobering thought when we consider that open doors are the means that give the demonic realm legal access.

But Jesus has an answer for you.

He has given you His mind, "the mind of Christ," to say no to temptation and yes to your new identity of purity. Under the New Covenant, His death, burial and resurrection empower you to close this door and to walk in healing and freedom.

YOU ARE JOINED TO JESUS

Here's some very good news: As a believer, you have been made holy, blameless, clean, and pure. You are joined to Jesus! You are one with Him, and your body is the temple of the Holy Spirit.

You know God, and because of this, it's time to learn a more excellent way:

> *It is God's will that you should be sanctified: that you should avoid sexual immorality; that each of you should learn to control your own*

> *body in a way that is holy and honorable, not in passionate lust like the pagans, who do not know God.*
> 1 Thessalonians 4:3-5

Let's close the door to sexual sin and break all ungodly soul ties. It's time to repent of the actions and behaviors of these destructive patterns that bring misery and shame, and to forgive those who have hurt you. It's time to embrace the truth of what God says about you, receiving His grace so you can walk in victory and purity. Your Father wants to meet your deepest relational needs and teach you what healthy nurturing looks like so that you can have profound and appropriate relationships with others.

You are an expression of the oneness of God!

CLOSE THE DOOR AND TAKE BACK YOUR POWER

Pray:

Father God, I thank You that I am Your child. I thank You that You will reveal destructive patterns in my life that hinder our relationship. I trust You. My focus is on You.

Ask:

Father God, show me how this door was opened. When did I begin to sin sexually, and is there any way in which I am still engaging in sexual sin? Help me to understand my behavior and what needs I am trying to meet through it.

Confess and repent:

Father God, I confess and repent of (name the specific sins as He reveals them to you). I receive and embrace Your forgiveness and cleansing.

Ask:

Father, is there anyone I need to forgive in relation to sexual sin?

Release forgiveness:

Father, I choose to forgive (say the person's name) for (say what they did or did not do) and for how it made me feel (be specific). I release them from my judgment and choose to bless them.

Break ungodly soul ties: This is where you get to sever any ungodly soul ties to individuals you had sex with outside of marriage. If you were involved with pornography or fantasy, be sure to break soul ties regarding that participation. Break any agreement you have made with the kingdom of darkness.

Father, with the sword of the Spirit, I sever all ungodly soul ties with (say the person's name). I cut myself free, take back what belongs to me, and release what belongs to them. Jesus, I renounce all forms of sexual sin and break any agreement I have made with the demonic realm behind this door. I command every enemy spirit to leave me now. I hand You all shame, guilt, and perversion. I shut and lock the door to sexual sin in my life. Holy Spirit, I ask You to fill me now in that place.

Ask:

Father, what would You like to give me in exchange?

6

The door to FALSE RELIGION & IDOLATRY

Inside this door can be found: *false religion, idolatry, magic, sorcery and witchcraft, occult video gaming, rebellion, yoga, Reiki, witchery and covens, necromancy, imaginary friends and spirit guides, hearing voices, secret pacts or vows, demonic and dark music, New Age, demonic manifestations, astrology, fortune telling, tarot cards, dark or secret initiations, Ouija and pendulum boards, séances, casting spells and curses, satanic rituals, fantasy and escapism, lying, deception, manipulation, intimidation, and any cults where controlling leadership taught that your voice has no value.*

Many people have been exposed to false religion and idolatry during their lifetime. One of the ways we identify false religion is by looking at the sense of power it creates in you—or takes from you.

You have been wired by the Father with a desire for greatness. Your need to feel powerful is a gift from Him because you were created to continue the ministry of Christ. God designed you to partner with Him to bring heaven to earth just like Jesus did. As Jesus was preparing to face the cross, He told the disciples, ". . .whoever believes in me will do the works I have been doing, and they will do even greater things than these" (John 14:12). What kind of works had Jesus done up to that point? He had declared and revealed the Kingdom by performing signs and wonders, raising the dead, healing people, and casting out demons. Jesus represented His Father's heart to the world by doing what He saw His Father do and saying what He heard His Father say.

Now, through the indwelling work of the Holy Spirit, we get to do the same. Our need for greatness is satisfied in a God-honoring way as the realities of heaven are released through us. Where there is sickness, we release healing. Where there is chaos, we release peace. Where there is anger, we release forgiveness. Where there is deception, we release truth. In short, we are commissioned to generously dole out the benefits of heaven just like Jesus did. What an invitation and a privilege!

This calling to continue the works of Jesus forms a foundational truth about our identity and purpose on earth. But if we don't fully believe it, we will try to meet our need for greatness in an ungodly way, opening the door to false religion and idolatry.

OPENING THE DOOR OF FALSE RELIGION & IDOLATRY

There are any number of ways this door could have opened in our lives, some of which appear religious, while others do not. The common factor is a misplaced desire for power. For example, participation in the occult or paranormal activities is often driven by the desire for special knowledge, power, or control. The desire itself may be normal and healthy, but when we seek to satisfy it through a supernatural source other than God, this door to idolatry is flung wide open.

Think back over your life. Perhaps you have been attracted to fantasy-based video games, or sought out hypnotism, palm reading, or astrology. You may have dabbled with a séance or an Ouija board at a slumber party as a child, or maybe as an adult seeking answers to the issues you were facing, you went to a fortune teller for advice or to have tarot cards read. Some of these actions may seem innocent and harmless, but the truth is, when you engaged in them, you opened a door whether you realized it or not, whether you meant to or not. The enemy is an opportunist—if he can get a foothold in your life when you are young and naïve, he will take it!

It doesn't matter if you simply played a game, were just curious about the New Age, or even went so far as to join a cult, practice witchcraft, or even make a vow to the devil—as long as this door of false religion and idolatry remains open in your life, it will block and limit your ability to truly connect with Jesus.

False religion and idolatry are counterfeit expressions of God's supernatural reality, and they belong to the kingdom of darkness. You do not reside there anymore! You are not to be under the influence of these fraudulent powers. Jesus desires to help you shut this door for good so you can enjoy unhindered intimacy with all three members of the Trinity.

YOU ARE A POWERFUL AGENT OF LIGHT

As a believer, you have been called out of darkness and into the light. The Bible makes this clear:

> *This is the life-giving message we heard him share and it's still ringing in our ears. We now repeat his words to you: God is pure light. You will never find even a trace of darkness in him. If we claim that we share life with him, but keep walking in the realm of darkness, we're fooling ourselves and not living the truth. But if we*

> *keep living in the pure light that surrounds him, we share unbroken fellowship with one another, and the blood of Jesus, his Son,* **continually** *cleanses us from all sin.*
> 1 John 1:5-7 (TPT)

Your heavenly Father dwells in perfect light, and when you received Christ as your Savior, He supernaturally transferred you into His light so you could enjoy permanent and unbroken fellowship with Him. Ephesians 5:8-11 (TPT) tells us:

> *Once your life was full of sin's darkness, but now you have the very light of our Lord shining through you because of your union with him. Your mission is to live as children flooded with his revelation-light! And the supernatural fruits of his light will be seen in you—goodness, righteousness, and truth. Then you will learn to choose what is beautiful to our Lord. And don't even associate with the servants of darkness because they have no fruit in them; instead, reveal truth to them.*

This is good news! You are joined to Jesus—there is not a hint of darkness in you, because Jesus does not live in dark, dirty places. He has made you completely clean, and enabled you to not only dwell in His light, but to shine with it yourself! This allows people to be drawn to you, not because you have assumed a counterfeit identity based on fantasy, but because of who you now are in Christ. You do not need to pretend—you *are* a new creation, with access to His supernatural Kingdom, and through your connection to Him you have become a powerful agent of supernatural light to the world around you. That means your mission is to release His light to those who are still in darkness. You are called to minister to those who are sick and oppressed—those who have any kind of lack in their lives—and to bring the reality of heaven to them.

Let's close the door of false religion and idolatry and embrace the truth of our identity in Christ. It's time to repent of any involvement you have had with false religion or idolatry, step fully into the light of God, and become a vessel of His power and authority, effectively and joyfully living out your purpose.

You are an expression of the greatness of God!

CLOSE THE DOOR AND TAKE BACK YOUR POWER

Pray:

Father God, I thank You that I am Your child. I thank You that You will reveal destructive patterns in my life that hinder our relationship. I trust You. My focus is on You.

Ask:

Father God, please show me how this door was opened in my life. When did I first participate in false religion and idolatry, and are there any openings to them in my life still? Help me to understand my behavior and what needs I am trying to meet through it.

Confess and repent:

Father God, I confess and repent of (name any specific sins). I receive and embrace Your forgiveness and cleansing.

Ask:

Father, is there anyone I need to forgive in relation to false religion and idolatry?

Release forgiveness:

Father, I choose to forgive (say the person's name) for (say what they did or did not do) and for how it made me feel (be specific). I release them from my judgment and choose to bless them.

Break ungodly soul ties: Sever any ungodly soul ties to individuals with whom you have participated in false religion and idolatry. Break agreement with the kingdom of darkness.

Father, with the sword of the Spirit, I sever all ungodly soul ties with (say the person's name). I cut myself free, take back what belongs to me, and release what belongs to them. Jesus, I renounce all participation with false religion and idolatry and break agreement with the demonic realm behind it. I command every enemy spirit to leave me now. I shut and lock the door to false religion and idolatry in my life. Holy Spirit, I ask You to fill me now in that place.

FALSE RELIGION & IDOLATRY

Ask:

Father, what would You like to give me in exchange?

7

The door to HATRED & ANGER

Inside this door can be found: *hatred, anger, rage, unforgiveness, rebellion, resentment, being offended, hostilities, swearing, being judgmental, bitterness, complaining, violence, prejudice, bigotry, envy, divorce, competition, selfish ambition, gossiping, slander, rejection, failure, guilt, jealousy, greed, materialism, deception, lying, quarreling, fighting, self-hatred (low self-worth), eating disorders, self-mutilation and cutting, hopelessness, depression, suicide, murder, and abortion.*

At some point in time, we have all experienced the feeling of anger. Like any other emotion, anger in itself is not wrong—often, it is a natural response to a wrong suffered. But anger generally leads to sin because it begins when we feel personally offended by what someone said or did to us. The truth is, whether the offense was real or perceived, something about it hurt. When we're offended, we often feel personally attacked. We become vulnerable to the words and actions of others, and our reactions can range from embarrassment to shame to outright anger and even hatred.

When we harbor anger in our lives, it festers and causes us to behave in ways that Paul warned us against in Galatians 5—our lives become marked by hostility, strife, jealousy, outbursts of anger, selfish ambition, dissensions, factions, and envy. These behaviors indicate that the door of hatred and anger has been opened in our lives.

IDENTIFYING THE DOOR OF HATRED & ANGER

When we're hurt, we look for someone to blame. We want someone to pay, someone to feel the pain we feel. In short, we want justice for the wrong done to us. But this need for justice, when not entrusted to the Lord, opens the door to hatred and anger, and left unresolved, anger will eventually lead to bitterness. Bitterness always causes trouble, defiling not only us but also those around us (Hebrews 12:15). Until we close the door of hatred and anger, this root of bitterness and unforgiveness will affect us physically, emotionally, spiritually, and relationally. In other words, it will impact every aspect of our being.

Our pain presents us with two choices: We can open the door of hatred and anger, creating destructive patterns of sin through our choices, beliefs and actions, or we can go directly to the Lord with our feelings, trust Him with the things done against us, and allow the Holy Spirit to bring healing.

It's that simple. *Really.*

But I can already hear you saying it: *You just don't know how much they hurt me.* This is true—I don't know the things that have hurt you, but thankfully, Jesus does. He is grieved by the pain you have experienced. But He is also grieved over the damage that anger is doing to you. And so He invites you to trust Him to show you a better way: Forgiveness.

THE WAY OF FORGIVENESS

I have ministered to hundreds of people who have spent years struggling to forgive those who hurt them. They've held onto their offense using sayings like: "Well, it was unfair," "It was not right," or "They don't deserve to be forgiven." I've been able to help them embrace the way of forgiveness, but this has only been possible by first ensuring they have a right understanding of what forgiveness is and isn't.

Forgiveness does not mean that what was done to you was justified, or that you feel great about what happened to you. Nor does it mean that you give up all your rights and the offending party gets off free; it is not about forgetting, condoning, or perpetuating injustice. What forgiveness does mean, is that you release another from your judgment and give God permission to render justice on your behalf. You cease your attempts to get justice through punishment and step out of the way to allow God to have a direct line to that person without your interference. In doing so, you are relieved of the heavy burden you have been carrying and freed from a prison of torment. The door is closed, and the enemy can no longer have access to your life.

It's also important to understand that forgiveness does not always result in reconciliation. Sometimes, that is neither wise nor possible. This is because trust and forgiveness are not the same. Trust must be earned. When it is lost, it must be restored. Forgiveness was established by Jesus as a non-negotiable practice for believers. *We forgive because we have been fully forgiven.* But that does not mean you must once again trust the person who violated you. Instead, we put our trust in God. When we forgive, we close the door of inner turmoil and open the door of His deep love for us. And in His love, we find our healing and freedom.

BOUND BY UNFORGIVENESS

Refusing to forgive does not hurt the one who harmed you; it only hurts *you*. It binds you in a prison of inner torment and keeps the door of hatred and anger wide open, hindering the fullness of what God intended for you to know and experience. Jesus came to set you free from this bondage. In Luke 4:18, Jesus quotes this passage from Isaiah about Himself:

> *The Spirit of the Sovereign Lord is on me, because the Lord has anointed me to proclaim good news to the poor. He has sent me to bind up the brokenhearted, to proclaim freedom for the captives and release from darkness for the prisoners.*
> Isaiah 61:1

Why is there a distinction here between captives and prisoners? Captives are held because of something done *to them*, because of the wounding they experienced and the ungodly choices made as a response, whereas for prisoners, it is because of something done *by them*—they deserve to be imprisoned. But both captives and prisoners need to know freedom. And whether they are bound because of what has been done to them or because of what they themselves have done, forgiveness is the key that will unlock the door of their prison cell.

If you are imprisoned by hatred and anger, you are the only one who can get yourself out of jail. Forgiveness is not about the other person; it is always about us. So don't wait until you feel like forgiving. Forgiveness is a decision of our will; it is a legal matter, not an emotional one. Ultimately, it is about our willingness to be obedient, because forgiveness is not an optional extra; for the believer, it is a command, a way of life. We are to forgive because we have been fully forgiven. The apostle Paul wrote:

> *Stop being mean, bad-tempered, and angry. Quarreling, harsh words, and dislike of others should have no place in your lives. Instead, be kind to each other, tenderhearted, forgiving one another, just as God has forgiven you because you belong to Christ.*
> Ephesians 4:31-32 (TLB)

Through the death, burial and resurrection of Jesus, you have been forgiven for every sin—past, present, and future! God holds nothing against you—

ever. Likewise, you are to stop holding bitterness against those who have hurt you. It's time to get out of jail. It's time to close the door of hatred and anger for good and start enjoying a deeper relationship with your Father who loves you. Embrace His total forgiveness and release it to others.

You are an expression of the mercy of God!

CLOSE THE DOOR AND TAKE BACK YOUR POWER

Pray:

Father God, I thank You that I am Your child. I thank You that You will reveal destructive patterns in my life that hinder our relationship. I trust You. My focus is on You.

Ask:

Father God, please show me how this door was opened. When did bitterness, anger, and unforgiveness enter my life, and is there any way in which I am still carrying these things? Help me to understand my behavior and what needs I am trying to meet through it.

Confess and repent:

Father God, I confess and repent of (name the specific sins). I receive and embrace Your forgiveness and cleansing.

Ask:

Father, is there anyone I need to forgive in relation to hatred and anger?

Release forgiveness:

Father, I choose to forgive (say the person's name) for (say what they did or did not do) and for how it made me feel (be specific). I release them from my judgment and choose to bless them.

Break ungodly soul ties: Sever any ungodly soul ties with individuals whom you have harbored anger, hatred and unforgiveness towards. Break any agreement you have made with the kingdom of darkness.

Father, with the sword of the Spirit, I sever all ungodly soul ties with (say person's name). I cut myself free, take back what belongs to me, and release what belongs to them. Jesus, I renounce all participation with this ungodly door and break agreement with the demonic realm behind it. I command every enemy spirit to leave me now. I hand You all bitterness, hatred, and anger. I shut and lock the door to hatred and anger in my life. Holy Spirit, I ask You to fill me now in that place.

Ask:

Father, what would You like to give me in exchange?

8

The door to FEAR & CONTROL

Inside this door can be found: *fear, need to control, worry, unbelief, anxiety, isolation, food additions, alcohol and drug addictions, tobacco and prescription addictions, revelry, escape, shoplifting, cheating, rejection, reoccurring nightmares, abandonment, shutting down, self-strength, pride, intimidation, fear of man, performance mindset, drivenness, perfectionism, seeking approval and acceptance, lying, exaggerating, deception, apathy, laziness, procrastination, and fear of failure.*

When I was nine years old, my home was completely destroyed by one of the worst tornado outbreaks in the South. Thankfully we were not in the house when it happened, but it was devastating nonetheless. We had been sent home early from school after a long day of storms and had taken cover a few miles away at my aunt's house. Eight adults and children sheltered in place there, off and on, for over ten hours. Then, just when it looked like the worst was over and we could safely return home, the tornado hit. Our home and neighborhood were demolished, and we lost everything.

I no longer felt safe, and for many years after, I was incredibly fearful of bad weather. The door to fear had been well and truly opened—not only for me, but also for my parents.

The door of fear is the primary door, the access point for the other three doors. Think of it like this: Opening the door of fear is like opening the front door to your house. Once the front door is open, you can then open all the other doors. This is the reason we shut this particular door last.

While fear can enter our hearts at any point in our lives, the door is usually first opened in our childhood. God wired us with a high need for love and protection, and He designed the family unit to be the primary place where these needs are met. But we live in a fallen world, and many parents have not dealt with their own heart issues. Perhaps they have not known how to get healing from the pain and wounds of their past or how to close destructive spiritual doors in their lives, and because of this, they are not always able to nurture and protect us as they should.

When our sense of security and control is taken from us, we try to fill the void with other things. Sometimes this looks like an over-developed sense of responsibility; we need to control all the things and all the people. Other times, we look as out of control as we feel on the inside—this is when we can have a tendency to commit the sins Paul warns us against in Galatians: drunkenness, carousing, and the like. Until this door of fear and control is closed, these cycles will continue from one generation to the next until someone decides that it ends with them.

This is where *you* come in! You may be the first person in your family to embrace heart-healing, stop destructive patterns of sin, and walk in the power Jesus has given you to live an abundant life. *The cycle can stop with you!* Today can mark a new beginning not only for you, but for all those you influence and who will come after you.

IDENTIFYING THE DOOR OF FEAR AND CONTROL

As we have ministered to countless people over the past two and a half decades, my team and I have found there are some common experiences the enemy uses to imprison people: *abandonment, rejection, and trauma.*

Trauma is an emotional response to a terrible event like an accident, a near-death experience, or a natural disaster. Immediately after the event, shock and denial are typical. Longer-term reactions include unpredictable emotions, flashbacks, strained relationships, and even physical symptoms like headaches or nausea. This was the case for my parents following the tornado. It took a real toll on them both. Consequently, tornadoes and storms were high on a list of triggers for them—something that was then passed on to me.

Trauma can also be the result of something ongoing that happened to us or around us—sickness, watching someone we love suffer, bullying, verbal abuse, and so on—or from the absence of something we needed but didn't get. This last type of trauma is often not as easily seen or identified. Such psychological, physical or emotional trauma stems from issues of neglect, abandonment, lack of affection or attention, the absence of age-appropriate limits, an unhealthy emotional environment in the home, or even a lack of being taught basic life skills.

Although these traumas are less visible to the human eye, they cause real damage, particularly during childhood, as they can impact the ability to develop a stable personality and the emotional capacity to process events.

Trauma can be classified as acute, chronic, or complex. Acute trauma results from a single incident, whereas chronic trauma is repeated and prolonged, as is often seen in cases of domestic violence or abuse. Complex trauma is where there has been exposure to varied and multiple traumatic events, often of an invasive, interpersonal nature.

Regardless of the cause or classification of our trauma, fear is often the result. In our pain event, we heard a subtle voice that said something like this: *This is really scary. I am afraid.* Our response was: *Yes, this is really scary. Yes, I am afraid.* In our agreement with fear, we inadvertently align with the enemy and empower his lies. When that agreement becomes a stronghold, we can find ourselves controlled by fear, even well into adulthood.

When we open the door to fear, we begin to behave accordingly—we choose to control, react, escape, medicate, and hide. These choices lead to a life of misery. Let's consider the core lies people tend to agree with so that we can find freedom from them. Consider which ones resonate with you:

- I am all alone
- I have to protect myself
- I am not loved
- I have to take care of myself
- Adults (or people) can't be trusted
- There is something wrong with me
- I'm always waiting for the next bad thing to happen

These lies often lead to questions like, *Why did God let this happen to me? Where was He? Why didn't God protect me? Doesn't He love me?* Without a solid foundation of truth in our lives, we will be tempted to answer these questions with more lies. But remember, when we partner with the voice of fear, we make ourselves susceptible to the other three spiritual doors.

Thankfully, Jesus has a solution! Since truth sets us free, we can bring the lies we have been believing before Him and ask Him to tell us His perspective. In other words, we can ask Him to exchange those lies with His life-giving truth!

This is what He did for me. One day, I invited Jesus into that place of pain and fear caused by the tornado. He changed everything for me in that moment. Now, when the weather gets a little crazy, I'm not rattled like I used to be, because my eyes are on Him. As I listen to His perspective about my situation, I keep this door of fear closed to the enemy, and ride out the storm with Jesus!

WRAPPED IN THE FATHER'S LOVE AND PROTECTION

King David modeled the power of meditating on truth when tempted to fear. He turned to the Lord to get His perspective, and in a time of warfare, heard this promise:

> *O Lord, you are my God and my saving strength! My Hero-God, you wrap yourself around me to protect me. For I'm surrounded by your presence in my day of battle.*
> Psalm 140:6a (TPT)

What was true for David is true for you also. God Himself has wrapped you in His eternal protection this side of heaven and beyond. He will never leave you, and He will never let anything take you away from Him. His presence always surrounds you, and His perfect love drives out every fear you face (1 John 4:18). In addition, your heavenly Father gives you this tremendous promise:

> *Everyone who loves the Lord and delights in him will cherish his words and be blessed beyond expectation . . . They will not live in fear or dread of what may come, for their hearts are firm, ever secure in their faith. Steady and strong, they will not be afraid, but will calmly face their every foe until they all go down in defeat.*
> Psalm 112:1, 7-8 (TPT)

The next time you are tempted to fear, pause, and bank on this promise. At the door of decision, cherish, meditate, and declare these words over yourself, believing without a shadow of doubt that you are secure in Him. Focus on His truth to keep you on the right path; the path of His love; the path that makes your heart firm, steady, and strong.

So let's close the door to fear. It's time to crawl up in the sheltered lap of your Father and become a receiver of His grace. He is the One who wired you for love and protection, and as your good Father, He desires to meet those needs entirely and wonderfully. He loves you as much as He loves Jesus (John 17:23)! Not only that, He *likes* you! When the Father looks at you, it's not through a filter of seeing Jesus first, as many have said. That sounds spiritual, but it's not biblical. Your Father looks directly at you because you are His child! He smiles and sings over you because you are part of His family. Your Father has seated you as close to Himself as you could possibly be this side of heaven (Ephesians 2:6). *He* is your safe place. Embrace these truths so that you can encounter a fresh revelation of His desire to nurture and bless you.

You are an expression of the lavish love of God!

CLOSE THE DOOR AND TAKE BACK YOUR POWER

Pray:

Father God, I thank You that I am Your child. I thank You that You will reveal destructive patterns in my life that hinder our relationship. I trust You. My focus is on You.

Ask:

Father God, please show me how this door was opened. When did fear and control enter my life, and is there any way in which they are still present? Help me to understand my behavior and what needs I am trying to meet through it.

Confess and repent:

Father God, I confess and repent of (name the specific sins). I receive and embrace your forgiveness and cleansing.

Ask:

Father, is there anyone I need to forgive in relation to fear and control?

Release forgiveness:

Release forgiveness to anyone with whom you are angry or from whom you have experienced pain.

Father, I choose to forgive (say person's name) for (say what they did or did not do) and for how it made me feel (be specific). I release them from my judgment and choose to bless them.

Break ungodly soul ties: Sever any ungodly soul ties with individuals who have made you feel unloved and unprotected, and break any agreement with the kingdom of darkness.

Father, with the sword of the Spirit, I sever all ungodly soul ties with (say the person's name). I cut myself free, take back what belongs to me, and release what belongs to them. Jesus, I renounce all participation with this ungodly door and break agreement with the demonic realm behind it. I command every enemy spirit to leave me now. I hand you all worry, anxiety, and fear, and I shut and lock the door to fear and control in my life. Holy Spirit, I ask You to fill me now in that place.

Ask:

Father, what would you like to give me in exchange?

A LETTER FROM VIKKI

Dearest Friend,

Take a couple of deep breaths. You did it! You *stepped up* and faced some hard stuff. You *stepped out* in faith to receive the Kingdom benefits of your new creation life.

Something powerful has just happened to you, and your life is forever changed. You have taken back your God-given authority.

You are likely feeling much lighter, more joyful, and have greater clarity. The destructive doors to the enemy have been closed, and the doorway to God's love and presence is wide open to you as a deeply loved son or daughter.

You can expect to experience life with lasting freedom as God intended now that sin's doors are properly addressed. Whenever you come to a doorway of decision, remember that you are able to make right choices—choices that reflect your true identity and enable you to enjoy a deeper relationship with Father, Jesus, and the Holy Spirit.

This new way of operating will take practice, but you have all you need to be powerful in Christ. Fix your eyes on Jesus, and determine to keep learning, growing, and pursuing the abundant life.

You are never alone. God is for you. Jesus is with you. Holy Spirit is in you.

Every Blessing, Vikki

ABOUT THE AUTHOR

As the founder of *Growing in Grace Ministries*, Vikki Waters has deep compassion for the healing and spiritual growth of others. Growing in Grace Ministries equips the body of Christ for abundant living, lasting freedom, and effectiveness in all they do.

In 1997, Vikki left a ten-year career in human resources to pursue God's call on her life for full-time ministry to His human resources, His beloved sons and daughters. Her desire is to declare and demonstrate the incredibly good news that Father God is in a good mood and is actively healing the brokenhearted, setting captives free, and lavishly releasing His love and favor on all who will receive!

Through her career as a businesswoman, civic leader and entrepreneur, Vikki understands the challenges of maintaining a healthy Christian lifestyle and applying godly principles in the workplace. She is a gifted teacher who will draw you close and hold you there while she encourages and inspires you to live and walk in the abundant life Jesus has for you. She is a woman you will love, as much for her contagious humor and warmth as for her tender heart and unashamed desire to live daily in the presence of the Lord.

Vikki's credentials and experience as a licensed ordained minister, author, hospital chaplain, Bible teacher, ministry trainer, guest teacher at Lee University, and heart healing coach, have made her a compelling and effective witness. But it is her heart that will reach you and draw you into God's presence.

Vikki and her husband, Richard, have been married for 37 years and live in Chattanooga, Tennessee. They enjoy spending time with their daughter, Emily, and her husband, Jack, and their grandchildren, John Morrison, Jacob Richard, and Lucy James.

STAY CONNECTED

I encourage you to read this book in a small group, Sunday School class, Bible study, book club, or with a close friend. Engage the Father's heart together and see where He takes those relationships! If you were blessed by this study, I would love to hear from you. Additional training, resources, and teachings are also available:

Website and Newsletter
www.vikkiwaters.com | www.growingingrace.today

Facebook
VikkiWatersMinistries | GrowinginGraceMinistries

Twitter
@VikkiWatersGGM

Instagram
@dr.vikkiwaters

Email
vikki@vikkiwaters.com

Podcast
Growing in Grace with Dr. Vikki Waters
www.growingingrace.today/podcast

SUPPORT AND JOIN THE HEART HEALING MOVEMENT

Get the Latest News
To stay connected and updated on all the latest content, resources, event dates and more, sign up for our newsletter.

Pray
We value and appreciate your prayers as we work to equip as many people as possible to experience abundant living, lasting freedom, and effectiveness in all they do.

Donate
Partner with some of our upcoming projects with a financial donation. Growing in Grace Ministries is a 501c3 non-profit. All donations are tax-deductible. Current projects include the creation of this Heart Healing Series, radio broadcasts, resource creation and translation, and mobile app development.

Receive Personal Ministry
Request a personal ministry session as an individual or a couple via Zoom. Ministry is issue-focused and aims to find the barriers hindering your personal connection with the Father, Jesus, and Holy Spirit. With a healed connection, you can walk in the destiny to which you have been called. Healed people heal people.

Join Growing in Grace Academy
A members-only community with empowering curriculums for heart healing, ministry training, and understanding the Bible as a whole through a better covenant perspective. Included in the membership are: core Bible studies, online courses, resources to grow every day, masterclasses, mentoring, curriculum, and community.

www.ingramcontent.com/pod-product-compliance
Lightning Source LLC
Chambersburg PA
CBHW050321010526
44107CB00055B/2339